Discover! 4

Animals In Art

Richard Northcott

Contents

WITHDRAWN From Toronto Public Library

D1113628

OXFORD
UNIVERSITY PRESS

OXFORD
UNIVERSITY PRESS

Great Clarendon Street, Oxford OX2 6DP

Oxford University Press is a department of the University of Oxford. It furthers the University's objective of excellence in research, scholarship, and education by publishing worldwide in

Oxford New York

Auckland Cape Town Dar es Salaam Hong Kong Karachi Kuala Lumpur Madrid Melbourne Mexico City Nairobi New Delhi Shanghai Taipei Toronto

With offices in

Argentina Austria Brazil Chile Czech Republic France Greece Guatemala Hungary Italy Japan Poland Portugal Singapore South Korea Switzerland Thailand Turkey Ukraine Vietnam

OXFORD and OXFORD ENGLISH are registered trade marks of Oxford University Press in the UK and in certain other countries

© Oxford University Press 2010

The moral rights of the author have been asserted

Database right Oxford University Press (maker)

First published 2010

2014 2013 2012 2011 2010

10 9 8 7 6 5 4 3 2 1

No unauthorized photocopying

All rights reserved. No part of this publication may be reproduced, stored in a retrieval system, or transmitted, in any form or by any means, without the prior permission in writing of Oxford University Press, or as expressly permitted by law,or under terms agreed with the appropriate reprographics rights organization. Enquiries concerning reproduction outside the scope of the above should be sent to the ELT Rights Department, Oxford University Press, at the address above

You must not circulate this book in any other binding or cover and you must impose this same condition on any acquirer

Any websites referred to in this publication are in the public domain and their addresses are provided by Oxford University Press for information only. Oxford University Press disclaims any responsibility for the content

ISBN: 978 0 19 464443 3

An Audio CD Pack containing this book and a CD is also available, ISBN 978 0 19 464483 9

The CD has a choice of American and British English recordings of the complete text.

An accompanying Activity Book is also available, ISBN 978 0 19 464453 2

Printed in China

This book is printed on paper from certified and well-managed sources.

ACKNOWLEDGEMENTS

Illustrations by: Kelly Kennedy pp.5, 6, 22, 42; Dusan Pavlic/ Beehive Illustration pp.24, 26, 46, 47; Alan Rowe pp.24, 25, 26, 29, 33, 40, 46, 47

The Publishers would also like to thank the following for their kind permission to reproduce photographs and other copyright material: Alamy pp.3 (Bernd Zoller/imagebroker/hare running, Durer, Albrecht (1471-1528)/The Art Gallery Collection/hare sitting), 7 (AfriPics.com/giraffes), 12 (Sculpture *Mother* by Louise Bourgeois/Ulana Switucha/© Estate of Louise Bourgeois. DACS, London/VAGA, New York 2010), 13 (Pep Roig/Gaudí Lizard), 16 (Helene Rogers/Art Directors & TRIP/stamp), 18 (The Print Collector/© ADAGP, Paris and DACS, London 2010); Akg-images p.6 (Bildarchiv Steffens); The Bridgeman Art Library pp.4 (*Study of a dog and a cat*, c.1480 (metalpoint on paper), Vinci, Leonardo da (1452-1519)/British Museum, London, UK), 5 (*Cats*, 17th century (ink on silk), Pyon Sang-Byok, (17th century)/National Museum, Seoul, Korea), 8 (*Monarch of the Glen*, 1851 (oil on canvas), Landseer, Sir Edwin (1802-73)/United Distillers and Vintners), 9 (*Tiger in a Tropical Storm (Surprised!)*, 1891 (oil on canvas), Rousseau, Henri J.F. (Le Douanier) (1844-1910)/National Gallery, London, UK), 11 (Snowman from series *Children's Games*, 1888 (colour woodcut), Eitaku, Kobayashi (1843-90)/© Central Saint Martins College of Art and Design, London) 11 (*Portrait of Jahangir holding a Falcon*, c.1600-10 (w/c & gold on paper), Manohar (fl.1580-1620) (attr. to)/Brooklyn Museum of Art, New York, USA/Gift of Mr. & Mrs. Robert L. Poster), 14 (The White Rabbit, illustration from *Alice in Wonderland* by Lewis Carroll (1832-98) adapted by Emily Gertrude Thomson (d.1932) 1889 (colour litho), Tenniel, John (1820-1914) (after)/Private Collection/Archives Charmet), 15 (*T03131 Turdus migratorius (American Robin) one male, two females and young*, engraved by Robert Havell II (1793-1878) plate CXXXI (131) from Audubon's *Birds of America* pub. 1832 (coloured engraving), Audubon, John Woodhouse (1812-62) (after)/ Natural History Museum, London, UK), 16 (Hieroglyphics, from the Tomb of Seti I, New Kingdom (wall painting), Egyptian 19th Dynasty (c.1297-1185 BC)/Valley of the Kings, Thebes, Egypt/Giraudon), 17 (H1945 Sheep, Chinese, 18th Century (soapstone),/© Oriental Museum, Durham University, UK), 19 (*Elephant, Horse and Cow*, 1914 (oil on canvas), Marc, Franz (1880-1916)/Private Collection), 21 (Children's toys: a hedgehog, a lion and a dove, Susa, Iran, Elamite Period, c.1150 BC (limestone and bitumen),/Louvre, Paris, France), 22 (*Sea Dragon* (coloured woodcut), Kunisada, Utagawa (1786-1864)/ Bibliotheque des Arts Decoratifs, Paris, France/Archives Charmet), 23 (*The Lady and the Unicorn: To my only desire* (tapestry), French School, (15th century)/Musee National du Moyen Age et des Thermes de Cluny, Paris/Lauros/Giraudon); Christy Crews Dunn/The Sylvan Gallery p.20 (teapot); Getty Images p.13 (Ken Straiton/First Light/totems); Oxford University Press p.17 and 33 (Chinese New Year symbols); Photolibrary p.7 (Yoshio Tomil Photo Studio/Aflo Foto Studio/monkey); Scala Archives p.10 (Detail of *Portrait of Don Manuel Osorio Manrique de Zuniga*, (1784-1792), oil on canvas, possibly c. 1790, Goya, Francisco de (1746-1828), Metropolitan Museum of Art, New York, image copyright The Metropolitan Museum of Art/Art Resource/ Scala, Florence).

Note for Parents and Teachers

The following works of art are pictured in the book but not named in the text:

p3 *A Young Hare* by Albrecht Durer (1502); p4 *Study of a dog and a cat* by Leonardo da Vinci (c.1480); p5 *Cats* by Pyon Sang-Byok (17th century); p8 *Monarch of the Glen* by Sir Edwin Landseer (1851); p9 *Tiger in a Tropical Storm (Surprised!)* by Henri J.F. Rousseau (1891); p10 *Portrait of Don Manuel Osorio Manrique de Zuniga* (detail) by Francisco de Goya (c.1790); p13 *Lizard in the Parc Güell, Barcelona* by Antoni Gaudí (1914); p11(top)

Snowman from 'Children's Games' by Kobayashi Eitaku (1888); p11(bottom) *Portrait of Jahangir holding a Falcon* attrib. to Manohar (c.1600); p14 *The White Rabbit* by John Tenniel, from Alice in Wonderland by Lewis Carroll, adapted by Emily Gertrude Thomson (1889); p15 *American Robins* by John Audubon (1832); p18 *The Seal* by Constantin Brancusi (1925); p19 *Elephant, Horse and Cow* by Franz Marc (1914); p22 *Sea Dragon* by Utagawa Kunisada (19th century); p23 *The Lady and the Unicorn: 'To my only desire'* by French School (15th century)

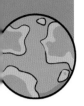

Introduction

Look at these two pictures of a hare. One is a photo, and the other is a painting. The photo is interesting, but in the painting the artist really helps us to look at the hare. We see its long claws, its fur, and its whiskers.

What animals do we see in art?
Where can we see animals in art?
What are the oldest animal pictures?

Now read and discover more about animals in art, all around the world!

Animal Shapes

Animals are different from people. Animals can't talk, but they can do many other things. Some animals can run faster than people. Most birds and insects can fly. Cats can climb trees better than people.

Here are drawings of a cat and a dog by an artist called Leonardo da Vinci. He was born in Florence, now in Italy. He wanted to show an animal's shape when it does different things. The dog is sitting. The cat is washing. Their shapes are interesting because they are different from ours.

Drawings of a Dog and a Cat

This painting is by a Korean artist called Byeon Sang-byeok. It shows two cats. The cats are not friends. Maybe they are going to fight. The artist shows this in their shapes. He used gray and black inks for the cats, to show their fur. Their fur is nice and soft.

Many artists draw pictures of animals because their shapes are interesting and beautiful.

A Painting of Two Cats

Discover!

Sometimes when artists paint animals, they first do a fast drawing. Then, later, they look at their drawing and do their painting more slowly.

→ Go to pages 24–25 for activities.

2 The Oldest Animal Pictures

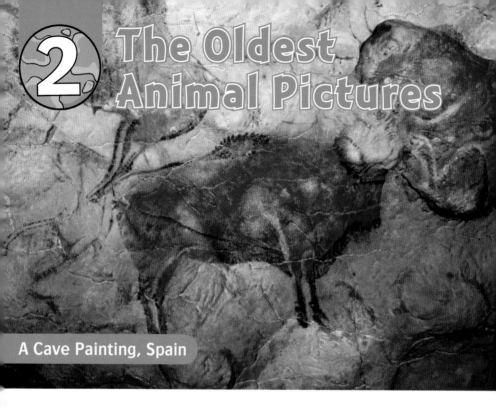

A Cave Painting, Spain

A long time ago, people lived in caves. They had no paper. They painted animals on the walls of their caves. In a cave in Spain, there's an amazing painting of a bison. This painting is about 15,000 years old.

Discover!

A girl called María Sanz de Sautuola discovered the cave paintings at Altamira in 1879. She was only nine years old. She was in the caves with her father.

There are beautiful paintings of giraffes and other animals in some caves in Libya. They are not as old as the cave paintings in Spain, but they are interesting because they show changes in our world. When people did these paintings, about 8,000 years ago, there were giraffes and trees in this part of Africa. Now it's a desert.

A Cave Painting, Libya

In the Nazca Desert in Peru you can see amazing pictures of animals, but you have to be in a plane. About 2,000 years ago, people drew giant pictures on the ground. They drew monkeys, birds, and spiders. Some of these pictures are bigger than a playground!

The Nazca Monkey, Peru

→ Go to pages 26–27 for activities.

Wild Animals

A Painting of a Stag

When artists paint a wild animal, they sometimes show the animal in its home. For example, they paint the animal in the jungle or in the mountains.

In this painting we see a stag, and we also see its home in the mountains. This painting is realistic. This means that the stag looks like a real stag – it's almost like a photo. The painting is by a British artist called Edwin Landseer. He painted it in 1851.

A Painting of a Tiger

In 1891, a French artist called Henri Rousseau painted a picture of a tiger. The painting is called *Tiger in a Tropical Storm (Surprised!)*. The artist shows the tiger and its home in the jungle.

Most of this painting is trees, other plants, and rain. We see a tiger, and we also see the tiger's world. The tiger is surprised because there's a storm. Do you think this is a realistic painting?

→ Go to pages 28–29 for activities.

People and Pets

Not all animals in art are wild animals. Some of them are people's pets.

Francisco de Goya was a Spanish artist. In about 1790, he painted a boy and his pets. The boy has a black and white bird on a piece of string. He also has some cats, and they are watching the bird. Paintings of people, like this painting, are called portraits. Francisco de Goya painted lots of portraits.

A Boy and His Pets

Pets in the Snow

This picture is by a Japanese artist called Kobayashi Eitaku. How many pets can you see? There's a dog and a rabbit, but is it a real rabbit?

A long time ago in India, rich people liked hunting with birds. In this painting, we see the emperor Jahangir and his pet falcon. They are going to hunt small animals. The artist used real gold to color some of the emperor's clothes.

Discover! This painting is very small. It's only 14 centimeters tall. Very small pictures like this are called miniatures.

Go to pages 30–31 for activities.

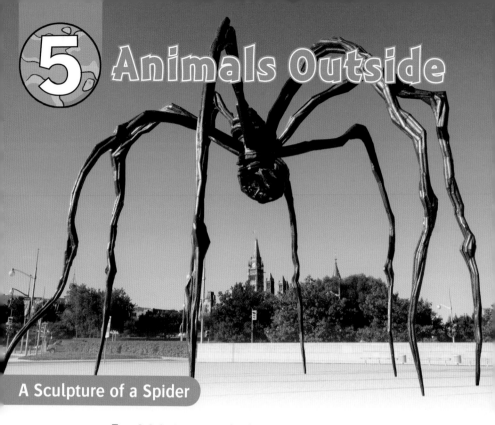

A Sculpture of a Spider

In 2005, people in Ottawa in Canada saw a spider next to a museum. Was it a small spider, like a spider in the bathtub? No, it was very big. This spider was a sculpture by an American artist called Louise Bourgeois. It was almost 10 meters high!

Louise Bourgeois was born in France in 1911. When she made this sculpture she was more than 90 years old. There are other big sculptures of spiders by Louise Bourgeois in Spain, Russia, and South Korea.

Native American artists make tall statues called totem poles. They put sculptures of birds and other animals on the poles. Totem poles are made of wood from very tall trees.

Discover!

The tallest totem pole in the world is in Alert Bay in Canada. It's about 56 meters tall.

A Statue of a Lizard

In Barcelona in Spain, there's a big statue of a lizard. Is this a realistic statue? Not really. When people see this lizard, they usually smile. It looks like a big toy.

Go to pages 32–33 for activities.

13

Animals in Books

Do you like learning about animals? Today we can watch animals on television, or look at photos of animals in books or on the Internet. A long time ago, before television or photos, people only looked at drawings of animals in books.

A Drawing of Alice's Friend, the Rabbit

There are often drawings of animals in children's books. In a book called *Alice's Adventures in Wonderland*, a girl called Alice meets a rabbit and lots of other animals. The drawings in this book are very nice, but they are not realistic because the animals are wearing clothes.

A long time ago, there were artists who studied animals from all around the world. They wrote books about them and drew the pictures in the books.

One of these artists was John Audubon. He was born in 1785 and he lived in the USA. He drew lots of birds and other animals.

Discover!

John Audubon drew all the different types of bird in North America, and he put the drawings in a book. This took 20 years.

Go to pages 34–35 for activities.

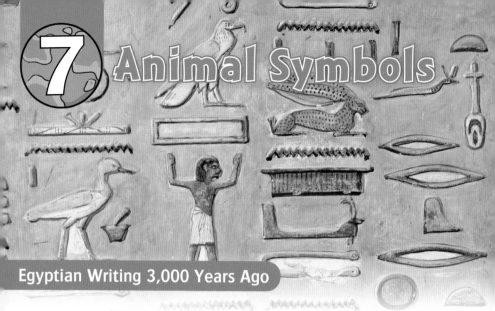

7 Animal Symbols

Egyptian Writing 3,000 Years Ago

A long time ago, people used pictures of animals in writing. In Ancient Egyptian writing, there are symbols of animals like birds and snakes. Sometimes the symbols mean the word for the animal. When they are next to another symbol, they can mean a different word.

A Rooster on a French Stamp

Animals are sometimes the symbols of countries. The tiger is the symbol of South Korea, and the rooster is the symbol of France. Sometimes you can see an animal symbol on a country's coins or stamps. Does your country have an animal symbol?

In China, all the years have an animal symbol. There are 12 symbols. For example, the Year of the Rabbit was from 1999 to 2000. The Year of the Sheep was from 2003 to 2004. These animal symbols can also mean different types of people. For example, people who are born in the Year of the Rabbit are kind. Do you think it's true?

This Chinese sculpture of a sheep looks like a real sheep. Maybe the artist made it because people who are born in the Year of the Sheep are good at art!

A Sculpture of a Sheep

→ Go to pages 36–37 for activities.

8 Different Animals

Animals in art are not always realistic. Sometimes artists have different ideas.

An artist from Romania called Constantin Brancusi made this sculpture of a seal in 1924. It's not a realistic sculpture, but the artist used a stone called marble to show his idea of a seal. The marble is gray, like a seal. It shines like a seal's fur when it's wet. The lines in the marble look like the water around the seal when it swims. The artist used hard, dry stone to show a soft, wet seal.

Discover!

Constantin Brancusi liked things made of stone. His table was a big piece of stone.

A Sculpture of a Seal

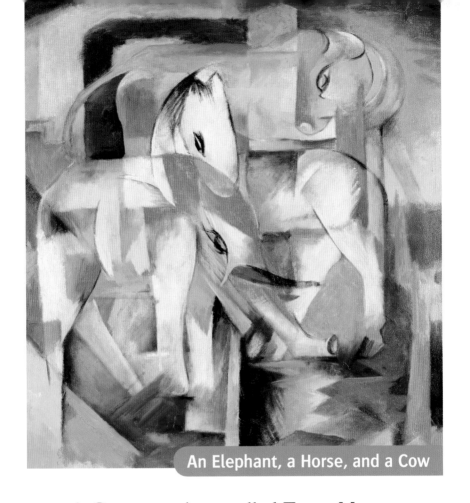

An Elephant, a Horse, and a Cow

A German painter called Franz Marc was interested in shapes and colors. In 1914, he painted a picture of an elephant, a horse, and a cow. Their colors are not realistic. The elephant's head is red, and part of the horse is blue. They are like animals in a dream. Franz Marc made a nice, colored pattern with the shapes of the three animals.

➔ Go to pages 38–39 for activities.

Teapots and Toys

It's fun to look at sculptures of animals in a museum, but usually you can't touch them. Sometimes, artists make things like teapots or toys with animal shapes. They are all animals in art, but you can touch them.

Here's a sculpture of a zebra. You can touch it because it's really a teapot. It's a teapot in the shape of a zebra. It's by an American artist called Christy Crews Dunn. She makes teapots in the shape of other animals, too.

A Zebra Teapot

bird

hedgehog

lion

Animal Toys

A long time ago, an artist made three little toys – a bird, a hedgehog, and a lion. All the toys had wheels. When young children play with toys, they often break them. The artist knew this, so these toys are strong. They are made of stone.

The artist lived in Susa, now in Iran. We don't know the artist's name. The bird doesn't have wheels now, but the toys look nice. They're about 3,000 years old, so they are some of the oldest toys in the world!

→ Go to pages 40–41 for activities.

10 Dragons and Unicorns

There are lots of stories and pictures of animals that aren't real, like dragons and unicorns. Sometimes they are more exciting than real animals.

A Picture of a Dragon

Dragons have long claws and their tails are like a lizard's tail. This Japanese dragon is long and thin, like a snake. It's big and angry. Maybe the people are scared.

Discover!

Japanese dragons always have three claws on each foot. In Ancient China, a dragon with five claws was the symbol of the emperor.

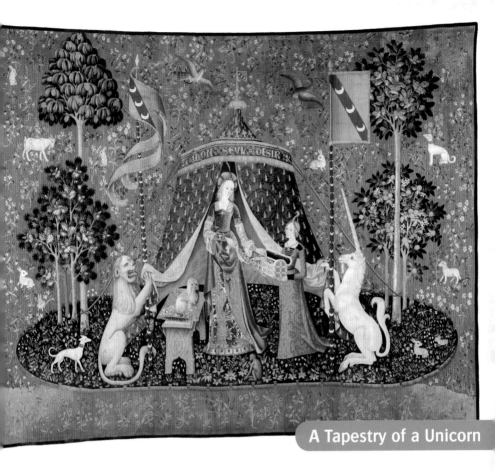

A Tapestry of a Unicorn

A unicorn looks like a white horse, but it has a horn on its head. In this old French tapestry, two women are with a unicorn. There are other animals, too. The animal in front of the women looks like a monkey. What other animals can you see?

Think about all the animals in this book. What's your favorite animal in art?

→ Go to pages 42–43 for activities.

1 Animal Shapes

← Read pages 4–5.

1 Write the words.

> fur   ~~artist~~   cat   dog   drawing   painting

1 ___artist___

2 _____

3 _____

4 _____

5 _____

6 _____

2 Circle the correct words.

1 Animals **can** / **can't** talk.

2 Some animals can **talk** / **run** very fast.

3 Most birds can **fly** / **talk**.

4 **Cats** / **Horses** can climb trees.

5 Cats have soft **fur** / **teeth**.

6 Fur is **hard** / **soft**.

3 **Read and draw.**

1 The dog is watching a cat.

2 The horse is running.

3 The monkey is watching a bird.

4 The lion is sleeping.

4 **Order the words.**

1 insects / fly. / Most / can

   Most insects can fly.

2 trees. / Cats / climb / can

   _____

3 fur. / cats / soft / Most / have

   _____

4 of / animals. / artists / draw / Many / pictures

   _____

5 Animal / different / are / shapes / from / ours.

   _____

② The Oldest Animal Pictures

← Read pages 6–7.

1 Write the words.

| bison | cave | desert |
| plane | giraffe | spider |

1 _____   2 _____   3 _____

4 _____   5 _____   6 _____

2 Write *true* or *false*.

1 People had books 15,000 years ago. _false_

2 There are paintings of bison in a cave in Spain. _____

3 A boy discovered the cave paintings in Altamira. _____

4 The Nazca Desert is in Spain. _____

5 There are cave paintings in Libya. _____

3 Match.

1 People painted animals on
2 A Spanish girl discovered
3 There's a big picture
4 Some pictures in the Nazca Desert
5 There are paintings of giraffes

of a monkey in the Nazca Desert.

are bigger than a playground.

the walls of caves.

in a cave in Libya.

the cave paintings at Altamira.

4 Answer the questions.

1 Where is Altamira?

Altamira is in Spain.

2 Who discovered the cave paintings in Altamira?

_____

3 Where is the Nazca Desert?

_____

4 What animals did people draw in the Nazca Desert?

_____

5 What animals are in the cave paintings in Libya?

_____

6 How old are the cave paintings in Libya?

_____

③ Wild Animals

← Read pages 8–9.

1 Complete the sentences.

jungle   French   tiger   mountains   stag   ~~British~~

1 Edwin Landseer was a ___British___ artist.

2 Henri Rousseau was a _____ artist.

3 Edwin Landseer's painting is of a stag in the

_____ .

4 Henri Rousseau's painting is of a tiger in the

_____ .

5 Edwin Landseer painted the _____ in 1851.

6 Henri Rousseau painted the _____ in 1891.

2 Match.

1 Are you from Spain?   Yes. I'm Polish.
2 Are you from South Korea?   Yes. I'm Russian.
3 Are you from Poland?   Yes. I'm English.
4 Are you from the USA?   Yes. I'm Korean.
5 Are you from England?   Yes. I'm Spanish.
6 Are you from Russia?   Yes. I'm American.

3 **Match the animals and their homes.**
Then write complete sentences.

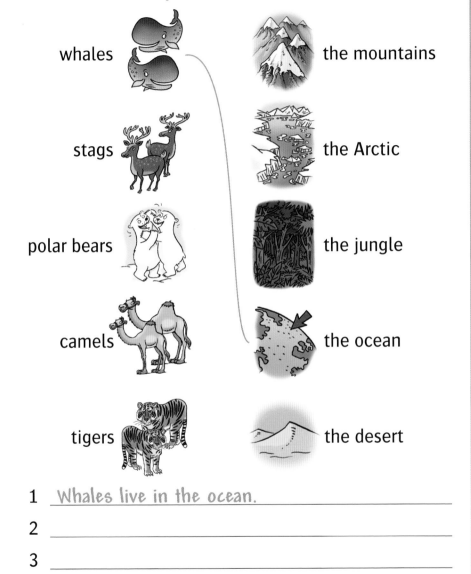

whales — the mountains

stags — the Arctic

polar bears — the jungle

camels — the ocean

tigers — the desert

1 Whales live in the ocean.

2 _____

3 _____

4 _____

5 _____

4 People and Pets

← Read pages 10–11.

1 Circle the odd one out.

1	bird	dog	(boy)	rabbit
2	black	bird	red	white
3	India	Korean	Spanish	Japanese
4	animal	hunt	watch	play
5	girl	emperor	pet	boy
6	painting	drawing	emperor	miniature

2 Read and draw.

1 The girl is with her horse.

2 The boy is holding a falcon.

3 The two cats are on the wall.

4 The man is holding his pet monkey.

3 Match.

1 Artists sometimes paint	a Spanish artist.
2 Francisco de Goya was	watching his bird.
3 The boy in the painting	people with their pets.
4 The boy's cats are	has a short tail.
5 The rabbit	has a black and white bird.
6 The dog	is made of snow.

4 Order the words.

1 Spanish / a / Francisco de Goya / artist. / was

_____

2 lots / of / He / painted / portraits.

_____

3 a / boy / He / his / pets. / and / painted

_____

4 The / bird. / has / boy / white / a / black / and

_____

5 two / also / has / He / cats.

_____

6 cats / the / bird. / The / are / watching

_____

5 Animals Outside

← Read pages 12–13.

1 Circle the correct words.

1 There **was** / **wasn't** a sculpture of a spider in Ottawa.

2 The spider was next to a **museum** / **river**.

3 The spider was almost **10** / **100** meters high.

4 Barcelona is in **France** / **Spain**.

5 There's a **portrait** / **statue** of a lizard in Barcelona.

6 Totem poles are **little** / **tall** statues.

2 Answer the questions.

1 Where is Ottawa?

_____

2 What did Louise Bourgeois make?

_____

3 Where can you see a statue of a lizard?

_____

4 What are totem poles made of?

_____

5 Where is the tallest totem pole in the world?

_____

3 Complete the sentences.

making   painting   taking

1 He's _____ a photo of a cat.

2 She's _____ a sculpture of a bird.

3 He's _____ a picture of a tiger.

4 Draw and write.

1 _He's making a sculpture of a lion._

2 _____

3 _____

6 Animals in Books

← Read pages 14–15.

birds   drawings
drew   lots
Internet   realistic

1 Complete the sentences.

1 We can see photos of animals on the _____ .

2 A long time ago, people looked at _____ of animals in books.

3 There are _____ of animals in *Alice's Adventures in Wonderland*.

4 They are not _____ animals because they're wearing clothes.

5 A long time ago, artists studied animals and _____ pictures of them.

6 John Audubon drew lots of _____ .

2 Write *true* or *false*.

1 The drawing on page 15 is by John Audubon. _____

2 John Audubon lived in India. _____

3 He never drew animals. _____

4 He drew all the different types of bird in North America. _____

5 This took ten years. _____

3 Match.

1 A long time ago, people
2 They looked at
3 Some artists drew pictures
4 The rabbit on page 14 is
5 *Alice's Adventures in Wonderland*
6 Do you like

in children's books.

wearing clothes.

pictures of animals in books.

didn't have televisions.

watching animals on television?

is about a girl called Alice.

4 Add the words and write correct sentences.

1 A long time ago, people at animals in books.

(looked) A long time ago, people looked at animals in books.

2 Today we can watch on television. (animals)

_____

3 *Alice's Adventures in Wonderland* is a children's.

(book) _____

4 The on page 14 is looking at his watch. (rabbit)

_____

5 Do you the birds on page 15? (like)

_____

6 John Audubon was a artist. (good)

_____

7 Animal Symbols

← Read pages 16–17.

1 Write the words.

dog	monkey	tiger	rabbit
horse	sheep	rooster	snake

1 _____ 2 _____ 3 _____ 4 _____

5 _____ 6 _____ 7 _____ 8 _____

2 Circle the correct words.

1 There are **pictures** / **photos** of animals in Ancient Egyptian writing.

2 The symbol of **South Korea** / **France** is the rooster.

3 A country's animal symbol is sometimes on its **person** / **stamps**.

4 In China, all the years have an animal **symbol** / **coin**.

5 These animals can mean different types of **coins** / **people**.

3 Write complete sentences.

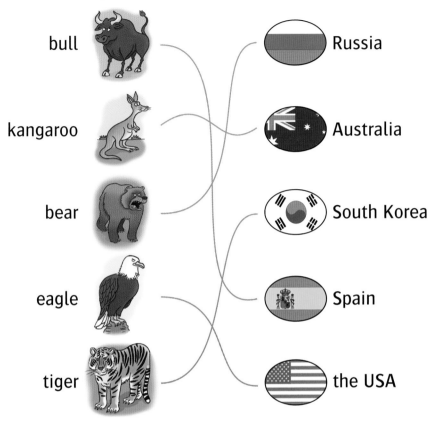

bull

kangaroo

bear

eagle

tiger

Russia

Australia

South Korea

Spain

the USA

1 <u>The bull is the symbol of Spain.</u>

2 _____

3 _____

4 _____

5 _____

4 Write about the symbol of your country.

_____

_____

(8) Different Animals

← Read pages 18–19.

1 Circle the odd one out.

1	red	horse	green	blue
2	Romania	China	Russia	Brancusi
3	elephant	horse	painting	cow
4	sculpture	realistic	statue	painting
5	marble	sculpture	painting	picture
6	horse	seal	photo	cow

2 Complete the sentences.

idea   table   realistic   Romania
artist   stone   seal   hard

1 Constantin Brancusi was an _____ .

2 He was from _____ .

3 In 1924, he made a sculpture of a _____ .

4 The sculpture isn't a _____ sculpture.

5 The artist shows his _____ of the seal.

6 The artist used _____ , dry stone.

7 Brancusi liked things made of _____ .

8 His _____ was a big piece of stone.

3 **Match. Then write sentences.**

Franz Marc was	is red.
He painted a picture of	a German painter.
The colors in his painting	are not realistic.
The elephant's head	three animals.

1 Franz Marc was a German painter.

2 _____

3 _____

4 _____

4 **Order the words.**

1 in / ocean. / Seals / live / the

_____

2 fast. / They / can / swim

_____

3 Franz Marc / a / German / was / painter.

_____

4 realistic. / isn't / painting / His / of / animals

_____

5 from / was / Romania. / Constantin Brancusi

_____

6 Do / sculpture? / his / you / like

_____

(9) Teapots and Toys

← Read pages 20–21.

1 **Complete the sentences. Then write the numbers.**

lion   ~~monkey~~   shape   wheels

1 This bag is in the shape of a ___monkey___ . ☐ 4

2 This teapot is in the _____ of a zebra. ☐

3 This horse has _____ . ☐

4 This _____ is made of stone. ☐

2 **Find and write the words.**

biteapototototoyirbirdyoghedgehogog

1 _teapot_____   2 _____

3 _____   4 _____

3 Match. Then write sentences.

The teapot on page 20 is	sculptures of animals.
The toys on page 21 are	in the shape of a zebra.
It's fun to look at	wheels.
Some old toys have	about 3,000 years old.

1 _____

2 _____

3 _____

4 _____

4 Add the words and write correct sentences.

1 Look! It's a teapot in the of a zebra. (shape)

_____

2 It's by American artist. (an)

_____

3 These old are from Iran. (toys)

_____

4 We don't the artist's name. (know)

_____

5 Maybe they're the toys in the world. (oldest)

_____

6 You usually can't sculptures in a museum. (touch)

_____

10 Dragons and Unicorns

← Read pages 22–23.

body   claw   eye
head   horn   mouth
~~tail~~   wing

1 Write the words.

1 ___tail___   5 _____

2 _____   6 _____

3 _____   7 _____

4 _____   8 _____

2 Answer the questions.

1 How many claws does a Japanese dragon have?

_____

2 Which animal was the symbol of the emperor of

Ancient China?_____

3 What color are unicorns?

_____

4 Are there really dragons and unicorns in the world?

_____

5 Is there a lion in the tapestry on page 23?

_____

6 What other animals can you see in this tapestry?

_____

3 Find the animals in art. Complete the chart.

Animals	Type of Art	Page
1 cats	painting	5
2 seal		
3 spider		
4 giraffe		
5 lizard	statue	
6 zebra	sculpture	
7 rabbit		
8 unicorn	tapestry	
9 stag		
10 sheep		
11 dog	drawing	
12 tiger		
13 monkey		
14 dragon		
15 birds		

My Favorite Picture

1 **Choose your favorite picture in this book. Write notes.**

1 What page is it on? _____

2 What is the animal? _____

3 Is it a real animal? _____

4 Is it a realistic picture? _____

5 What colors and shapes can you see?

_____

6 What is the animal doing?

_____

7 Can you see the animal's home?

_____

8 Why do you like this picture?

_____

_____

2 **Draw your favorite picture in this book and write about it. Display your work.**

An Animal in Art

1 Find an animal in art. Look in books or on the Internet, or use a postcard.

2 Write notes.

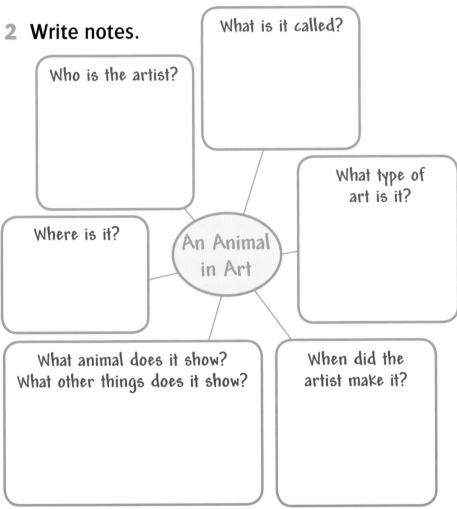

Who is the artist?

What is it called?

Where is it?

An Animal in Art

What type of art is it?

What animal does it show? What other things does it show?

When did the artist make it?

3 Make a poster. Write about your animal in art and add a picture. Display your poster.

Picture Dictionary

 artist

 bison

 claws

 clothes

 coin

 drawing

 emperor

 fur

 gold

 ground

 hard

 hare

 horn

 ink

 insects

 jungle

 museum

 painting

 pattern

 photo

    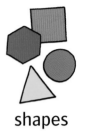

| portrait | rabbit | sculpture | seal | shapes |

sheep   snake   soft   spider   statue

stone   storm   symbols   tail   tapestry

teapot   unicorn   wheel   whiskers   wild animals

Oxford Read and Discover

Series Editor: Hazel Geatches • CLIL Adviser: John Clegg

Oxford Read and Discover graded readers are at four levels, from 3 to 6, suitable for students from age 8 and older. They cover many topics within three subject areas, and can support English across the curriculum, or Content and Language Integrated Learning (CLIL).

Available for each reader:
• Audio CD Pack (book & audio CD)
• Activity Book

For Teacher's Notes & CLIL Guidance go to
www.oup.com/elt/teacher/readanddiscover

Subject Area / Level	The World of Science & Technology	The Natural World	The World of Arts & Social Studies
3 — 600 headwords	• How We Make Products • Sound and Music • Super Structures • Your Five Senses	• Amazing Minibeasts • Animals in the Air • Life in Rainforests • Wonderful Water	• Festivals Around the World • Free Time Around the World
4 — 750 headwords	• All About Plants • How to Stay Healthy • Machines Then and Now • Why We Recycle	• All About Desert Life • All About Ocean Life • Animals at Night • Incredible Earth	• Animals in Art • Wonders of the Past
5 — 900 headwords	• Materials to Products • Medicine Then and Now • Transportation Then and Now • Wild Weather	• All About Islands • Animal Life Cycles • Exploring Our World • Great Migrations	• Homes Around the World • Our World in Art
6 — 1,050 headwords	• Cells and Microbes • Clothes Then and Now • Incredible Energy • Your Amazing Body	• All About Space • Caring for Our Planet • Earth Then and Now • Wonderful Ecosystems	• Helping Around the World • Food Around the World

For younger students, **Dolphin Readers** Levels Starter, 1, and 2 are available.